599.74   Ahlstrom, Mark E.
AHL
            The coyote

$10.95   9/91

DATE			

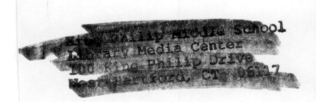

THE COYOTE

BY
MARK E. AHLSTROM

EDITED BY
DR. HOWARD SCHROEDER
**Professor in Reading and Language Arts
Dept. of Elementary Education
Mankato State University**

PRODUCED AND DESIGNED BY
BAKER STREET PRODUCTIONS
Mankato, MN

CRESTWOOD HOUSE
Mankato, Minnesota

LIBRARY OF CONGRESS CATALOGING IN PUBLICATION DATA

Ahlstrom, Mark E.
  The coyote.

  (Wildlife, habits & habitats)
  SUMMARY: Describes the physical characteristics, habits, and natural environment of the coyote and discusses its struggles for survival in the face of determined efforts by man to eradicate the species.
  1. Coyotes--Juvenile literature. (1. Coyotes) I. Schroeder, Howard. II. Title. III. Series.
  QL737.C22A33   1985   599.74'442   85-24290
  ISBN 0-89686-277-1 (lib. bdg.)

International Standard Book Number:	Library of Congress Catalog Card Number:
Library Binding 0-89686-277-1	85-24290

ILLUSTRATION CREDITS:

Lynn Rogers: Cover, 5, 6, 12, 24-25, 40
Wyman P. Meinzer, Jr.: 9, 11, 16, 20, 32, 35
Phil & Loretta Hermann: 19, 37, 44
John Shaw/Tom Stack & Assoc.: 23
Stephen Krasemann/DRK Photo: 26
Richard P. Smith/Tom Stack & Assoc.: 29, 42
Rod Allin/Tom Stack & Assoc.: 31
Lynn M. Stone: 39

CRESTWOOD HOUSE

Hwy. 66 South, Box 3427
Mankato, MN 56002-3427

TABLE OF CONTENTS

Some coyotes refuse to eat sheep

It was a big day for Carl Gustavson. He was about to see if his new idea would solve a big problem.

Carl grew up in the state of Utah. While still a young man, he developed an interest in wildlife. Later, he became an animal psychologist. He studied the reasons animals behave as they do. Carl's special interest was discovering how animals chose the foods that they ate.

As a scientist, Carl didn't think much of what sheep ranchers were doing to solve the problem they were having with coyotes. He could understand why the ranchers were upset. Coyotes were killing some of their sheep. But he didn't think that the method they were using to solve the problem was very smart.

For many years the U.S. government had spent millions of dollars trying to kill coyotes all over the western United States. War had been declared! The goal of the government, and the ranchers, was to get rid of all coyotes. The phrase, "the only good coyote, is a dead coyote," became very popular.

Over the years, several million coyotes were trapped,

4

"War" was declared on the coyote in the early 1900's.

The large-scale killing had little effect on the number of coyotes.

poisoned, or shot. A strange thing was happening, however. The killing was having very little effect on the numbers of coyotes that were roaming the land. In some areas, there were more coyotes than ever before. The coyotes were also getting harder to kill—they had learned how to avoid man and his poisons.

Carl Gustavson thought that he had found a better way to solve the problem. He had heard about work that other scientists were doing with an idea called "taste aversion.'' These scientists had found that if an animal gets sick after eating something, it will never eat that food again.

Carl knew that not all coyotes killed sheep. He also knew that coyotes helped ranchers by killing rodents and other small animals that can ruin land that sheep graze upon. Carl thought he had found a way for ranchers to have both coyotes and sheep on their land.

To test his idea, Carl needed coyotes to work with. He gathered seven coyotes that were live-trapped in the wild. The coyotes were between two and four years old. Most of them had been seen attacking lambs and rabbits before they were captured. Carl fed the coyotes nothing but dog food.

Then one day Carl fed a piece of lamb meat to each of the coyotes. The meat was treated with lithium chloride and wrapped in fresh sheepskin. Lithium chloride is a chemical that will make humans and animals vomit when they eat it. Carl hoped that his coyotes would develop a taste aversion to eating lambs.

This brings us back to the beginning of the story. Carl was about to see if his idea would work. One at a time the coyotes were turned loose in a pen with a lamb. The coyotes had not been fed for several days, so they were hungry. When the lamb walked up to one coyote, the coyote ran away. Another coyote vomited after getting a sniff of the lamb. None of the coyotes wanted anything to do with the lamb. Carl's idea seemed to work!

CHAPTER ONE:

The wily coyote

Anyone that has seen a Road Runner cartoon knows about the sly, crafty animal called Wily Coyote. When the writers of the cartoon chose to call the coyote wily, they hit the nail right on the head. There probably is no animal that is more sly and crafty than the coyote. But the writers also made a mistake. In the cartoon stories, the Road Runner always outsmarts the Wily Coyote. In real life, almost no one outsmarts the coyote.

For over one hundred years, people have been trying to get rid of the coyote. Millions upon millions of dollars have been spent in this effort. Since 1915 alone, professional hunters, hired by the U.S. Fish and Wildlife Service, have killed around four million coyotes. As no one kept track of the numbers before 1915, it's hard to say how many coyotes have been killed since "war" was declared on them in the 1860's.

If numbers of coyotes killed mean anything, victory should have been declared long ago. But despite man's best efforts, there are more coyotes than ever before. There's a lesson in this for all of us.

At home on the plains

Before the American West was settled, there was no coyote problem. Coyotes lived mainly on the open plains between the Mississippi River and the Pacific Ocean. Their range extended north onto the plains of south-western Canada, and south a ways into Mexico.

By day, the coyote hunted for prairie dogs and other small rodents. At night, it mainly hunted for jack rabbits that were out eating prairie grasses.

Whenever it found them, the coyote ate the leftovers of prey killed by larger predators. The larger predators,

The coyote often eats the leftovers of larger predators.

like the wolf and cougar (or mountain lion), were able to attack and kill large prey animals like the bison (buffalo), antelope, and deer. (Even wolves and cougars usually killed only the animals that were weak from sickness or old age.) Because the coyote was too small to kill such large prey, it had learned to wait until the larger predators had eaten their fill. Then the coyote would move in and eat the scraps.

Everywhere it lived, the coyote was treated with respect by Indian tribes. They noticed how clever the coyote was. Some tribes even thought that the coyote was a god. These tribes believed that when the earth got old, and all living things passed away, one animal would remain—the coyote. As we shall see, there may be more than a little truth in this legend.

The "barking dog"

When members of the Lewis and Clark Expedition of 1804, first saw a coyote, they thought it was some kind of fox. After getting a closer look, they decided it was a small wolf. Because it lived on the plains, they called it a "prairie wolf." When later explorers saw it in areas with low brush, they called it a "brush wolf." Many people just called them "little wolves."

The coyote was given its official name, *Canis latrans,* by a naturalist, Thomas Say. He was part of another

The coyote's official name is "Canis latrans."

group sent by the U.S. government to explore the West in 1819. While on the Missouri River, near what is now Council Bluffs, Iowa, Say saw his first coyote. Other members of the group called it a "prairie wolf." But after seeing more coyotes along the way, Say began to realize that the animal didn't behave like a wolf. He noticed that the coyote often seemed to be alone. Being a naturalist, he knew that wolves were usually in packs. Later, when he returned home to Philadelphia, Pennsylvania, he came up with a name. He decided to name this wild dog after its barking cry. *Canis latrans* means "barking dog."

The coyote is well known for its barking cry.

Thomas Say made this animal part of the wild dog family, known by scientists as *Canidae*. The other members of this family in North America are wolves and foxes.

The common term, coyote, comes from the Aztec Indian word for the same animal, *coyotl*. The Aztecs lived in Mexico. Early settlers in the southwestern U.S. picked up the term. The settlers changed *coyotl* to coyote, a word that would better fit the English language.

"The age of extermination"

Although early settlers were already trying to get rid of some coyotes, the coyotes' real troubles did not begin until 1862. With the passage of the Homestead Act of 1862, the U.S. government sold millions of acres of land in the West. The land was sold at very low prices. The government wanted people to settle the area.

Thousands of people took up the government's offer, and headed west. When they crossed the Mississippi River, they found that most of the land was not good for farming. It was too dry to raise crops. However, the rolling hills were covered with native grasses. The settlers decided that the land would be perfect for raising sheep and cattle.

But there was a problem. Great herds of bison lived

on the same prairie lands. The bison were grazing on the same grasses that the settlers wanted for their sheep and cattle. Herds of antelope, prairie dogs, and other grass-eating animals also lived on the prairie.

With the U.S. government's help, the settlers set out to get rid of any wild animal that ate grass. Thus began what historians have called "the age of extermination."

The government was most helpful when it came to getting rid of the bison. For the government knew that Indians also needed the bison to survive. If the bison could be exterminated, the war against the Indians would be all but over.

Professional hunters were hired to kill the bison. Market hunters joined in when they found that there was a market for the hides of the bison. (People in the eastern United States wanted the hides for their warmth. The "buffalo-skin robe" became very popular.) Even tourists shot the bison. Special trains brought the tourists on the new railroad tracks that had been laid west of the Mississippi River. The tourists shot the bison for fun. Most of the bison were left to rot. The same things happened to the bison herds on the plains areas of southern Canada.

No one knows for sure how many bison were killed. The best estimate is that about sixty million bison died before the killing stopped. A count was made of the bison remaining in 1891. There were 541 left in the United States, and 250 in Canada. The herd had come close to being exterminated. (Today, the only large herds are in government-owned parks.)

Antelope suffered the same fate. In the case of the antelope, the fences that the settlers had put up were just as effective as the market hunters. For some reason, antelope don't like to jump fences. Even though they could easily jump a fence, most antelope won't. The result was that the antelope were often cut off from their natural supply of water. The herds slowly died off.

Out of a herd that once numbered about fifty million, there were only about twenty thousand antelope left by the early 1900's. (Note: because of the efforts of concerned hunters and people of all kinds, there are almost one-half million antelope in the western U.S. today.)

The main weapon against prairie dogs and other small grass-eating animals was poison. Poison was put into the burrows of these animals. There was a special method used to kill jack rabbits. Great numbers of people would surround an area known to have jack rabbits. They would walk towards the middle of the area, and "close the ring." Then the rabbits would be clubbed to death.

A bigger problem

As these grass-eating wild animals were being killed, the settlers discovered that they had a bigger problem on their hands. With their natural prey gone, the wolves, cougars, and coyotes started killing cattle and sheep.

Now the settlers had to go after the predators. The professional hunters were able to get rid of most of the wolves and cougars by using poison. The usual method was to put poison, usually strychnine, on a dead calf or lamb. Sooner or later, some predator would find the animal, eat it, and die. Sometimes traps would be placed near the dead animals, too. Before long, there were very few wolves and cougars left on the prairies. The only ones that survive today live in remote areas, away from people.

But the coyote refused to leave. Gradually, the coyote learned to avoid eating dead livestock. To avoid traps, they learned to not even go near the dead animal. Nobody really knows how, or why. There is no doubt that thousands of coyotes were killed during the learning

Coyotes learned to be very careful around dead animals.

process. But they did learn. The coyote learned that it had to kill what it was going to eat. When they couldn't find any natural prey, coyotes once again were forced into killing domestic livestock. They usually went after chickens, lambs, and calves.

The settlers were also learning something. It seemed that whenever they settled in a new area, the coyotes moved with them. The coyotes followed settlers all across southern Canada. They followed settlers out of the plains and into the foothills of the mountains in Canada and the U.S. When cattle ranching became a big business in Mexico, the coyotes went south of the border in greater numbers. In fact, they went all the way to Central America.

Coyotes went north, too. During the Klondike Gold Rush of the late 1890's, the coyote followed people into the Yukon and Alaska.

Before long, most of the professional coyote hunters lost interest. Coyotes were becoming too clever. When the hunters couldn't kill the coyotes, they couldn't sell the hides or collect the bounties that were being offered. It was now up to other people to take care of the coyote problem.

The poisoning of the West

By the early 1900's, the settlers of the American West were known as ranchers. Many ranchers owned large areas of land, and they had become wealthy. They made a point of giving money to politicians. In exchange, the politicians watched after the ranchers' interests.

Much of the land that the ranchers owned was now ruined. They had been grazing too many sheep and cattle on the land. The animals had eaten the grass down to bare dirt. So the ranchers turned to the federal government for help. For a very small amount of rent, they were allowed to move their herds to the large areas of land still owned by the federal government.

Then the ranchers said that the coyotes were becoming a big problem on the federal land. They asked the government to do something about it.

Many biologists working for the government didn't think it would be smart to kill coyotes. They pointed out that coyotes eat rabbits and other small animals that eat a lot of grass—grass that is needed by sheep and cattle. In short, these biologists thought that killing coyotes might make the problem worse. The biologists also pointed out how hard it was getting to kill coyotes.

But the ranchers got their way. The U.S. Fish and Wildlife Service was put in charge of a "predator control program." The Wildlife Service set up a new division called the Predator and Rodent Control Agency to do the work. This agency hired hundreds of people to do the actual killing. Their job was mainly to shoot, poison, and trap coyotes on federal land. Although these people, called "government trappers" at first, used many methods to kill coyotes, their main weapon was

Over the years, millions of coyotes have been killed and left to rot.

poison. They thought that poison would be the easiest way to kill coyotes.

For fifty years, from 1920 to 1970, the Wildlife Service used poisons of all kinds on public lands. They used old poisons, like strychnine. They used new poisons like Compound 1080. As the coyotes caught on to the old method of putting poisons in dead animals and chunks of meat, the trappers were forced to try new methods.

New methods are tried

One of the new methods was to form strychnine into pellets. The pellets were then coated with sugar and lard

"Government trappers" kept trying new methods to kill the clever coyote.

to make them tasty to coyotes. Millions of these pellets were dropped all over the western United States. The trappers used trucks, trail bikes, and even airplanes to spread the pellets.

Another method of getting poison into a coyote was the "coyote getter." The heart of the coyote getter is an explosive cartridge. The cartridge contained poison, and was fastened to a stake with a short piece of wire. The whole thing was covered with sheep or rabbit fur. Sometimes the fur would be soaked with scents to make it more attractive to coyotes. When a coyote pulled on the fur, the posion cartridge exploded in its mouth.

There was a problem with the original coyote getter. It was dangerous. Many trappers were injured when the "getters" exploded as they were being set up. One person was killed when poison entered his body through the wound made by the explosion. Because of these problems, a new coyote getter was developed. The new "getters" use a strong spring to shoot poison into a coyote's mouth.

People get worried

All of these methods were killing a lot of coyotes. But people began to be concerned about the side effects of all the poison. Many animals besides coyotes were being killed. Pet dogs and cats were dying. Dead bald eagles were found.

To calm people's fears, the U.S. Fish and Wildlife Service changed the titles of the people that were doing the killing. The government trappers became "mammal control specialists." When enough people discovered that "control" really meant killing, the title was again changed. Today, the people that kill coyotes are called "district field assistants." The Predator and Rodent Control Agency has become the Division of Wildlife Services. If it weren't such a deadly business, all of this name-changing would be almost funny.

Many cattle and sheep ranchers also got worried about the government's program. Beginning in the 1950's, some of the ranchers started to protect the coyote! They saw that killing coyotes only made things worse. They were being overrun by rats, mice, and grass-eating rodents. The ranchers were also worried about the effects of all the poison on wildlife of all kinds. These ranchers asked the "district field assistants" to stop killing coyotes.

But man's "war" on the coyote still goes on in some areas. Many ranchers still think that it is smart to kill coyotes, so the killing continues. The Division of Wildlife Services is now more careful about which poisons it uses. It is also more careful about how the poisons are used.

Some ranchers are trying ideas like Carl Gustavson's.

Many ranchers now welcome the coyote.

If these new methods work, the ranchers will have the best of all worlds. The coyotes would stop killing their livestock, and still be around to eat grass-eating rodents and other pests. And most importantly, the poisoning of the earth could stop.

In the meantime, the coyote has been busy expanding its range. Beginning in the 1930's, the coyote started moving into the eastern United States. It is now believed that there are at least a few coyotes in every state east of the Mississippi River. Many of these states have a lot of coyotes.

The coyote now has the largest range of any wild animal in North America.

Despite all the killing, the coyote now has the largest range of any wild animal in North America. There are more coyotes than ever before. They are found in Death Valley, California, where temperatures reach 135 °F. They are found on the plains of Canada, where temperatures can drop to −60 °F in the winter. And they are found almost everywhere else in between. Experts think that there may be as many as two thousand coyotes within the city limits of Los Angeles, California!

In an effort to see how this is possible, let's take a look at some of the coyote's habits.

Some coyotes now live very close to populated areas.

CHAPTER TWO:

A very smart animal

Despite man's best efforts to kill it off, the coyote has survived. If you think this means that the coyote is smart, you're right.

Through experience, biologists have discovered a good way to tell how smart an animal is. They watch the adults go about their day-to-day business. If adult animals make a habit of playing, biologists know that the animals are smart. Members of the ape family, porpoises, and pet dogs have this habit. All of the wild dogs (foxes, wolves, and coyotes) play as adults. None of the wild dogs play more than the coyote. Adult coyotes have been seen playing with other kinds of animals, and even birds. They will also chase things just as a kitten does. They have been seen playing with stones, leaves, and mice. Adult coyotes often play with each other.

A clever hunter

Coyotes will sometimes work in pairs when hunting jack rabbits. The coyotes seem to know that jack rabbits have a habit of running in circles when chased. One coyote will chase the jack rabbit. The other coyote will hide where the chase started. When the rabbit returns to its starting point, the second coyote will be waiting.

When chasing larger prey, like an antelope, coyotes will sometimes run in relays. A group of three or four coyotes will take turns running. The coyotes force the antelope to run in a circle past the group. When one coyote gets tired, another coyote takes its place. Sooner or later the antelope will drop from exhaustion.

Many times, coyotes have been seen hunting with badgers. When the badger starts digging in the burrow of an animal that lives underground, the coyote will sit by an escape exit. If the animal is scared by the badger's digging, it will try to leave by the "backdoor." The coyote will be waiting.

When the ground is covered by deep snow, coyotes will follow elk herds. After the elk have pawed away the snow to get at the grass, the coyotes move in. It is now much easier for them to find mice, one of their favorite foods.

We'll probably never really know how smart any wild animal is. But it's no wonder that biologists think that no wild animal is any better at using its brain than the coyote.

Coyotes eat almost everything

All wild dogs are classified as "carnivores," or meat-eating animals. But all wild dogs are, in fact, "omnivorous"—they eat both plants and animals. No wild animal is better than the coyote when it comes to eating just about anything that crosses its path. It eats berries and fruits of all kinds. The coyote especially likes watermelons. A couple of coyotes can make a mess out of a melon patch in a hurry. They have a habit of only taking a bite or two out of each melon.

We already know that coyotes eat domestic livestock if they have to do so. But they prefer natural foods.

This coyote is eating wild raspberries.

29

They will kill and eat many kinds of small wild animals. Coyotes will also eat large wild animals that have been hit by cars or died from natural causes.

A biologist, Adolph Murie, did a study on coyotes living in Yellowstone National Park in 1937. Murie wanted to find out what the coyotes were eating. This was during the middle of the great effort to exterminate the coyote. People thought that coyotes were killing off the herds of game animals in the park. They also thought that the coyotes were leaving the park to kill ranchers' livestock. Murie watched the coyotes for two years.

The only big-game animals that Murie saw coyotes kill were old or sick. He found that they had no need to leave the park to feed on domestic livestock. To find out exactly what the coyotes ate, he collected their droppings. He carefully took thousands of droppings apart. Murie found that the major part of the coyote's diet was small animals. Mice and pocket gophers were the most common. He also found some surprising things in the droppings. In addition to the common game animals, he found bits of bat, house cat, ducks, owls, bird eggs, snakes, beetles, crickets, snails, seeds, mushrooms, and pine nuts.

Murie also found bits of things that only a coyote could explain. He found leather, cellophane, banana peels, mud, a shoestring, a lemon rind, a match, and part of a gunny sack. It would appear that the coyote does eat just about everything!

Hunting habits

The coyote needs two to three pounds of food every day. Most of its hunting is done in the cool of the early evening, or at night. If it is still hungry, the coyote will also hunt during the daytime. It will spend more time hunting during daylight hours in the winter, because food is harder to find. After the coyote has eaten its fill, it will rest in the shelter of a bush, large rock, or cliff.

More time is spent hunting during the day in winter. This coyote is waiting to pounce on a mouse it has heard under the snow.

31

Coyotes often hunt together.

Coyotes will often hunt in pairs, and sometimes in groups of three or four. They usually hunt along favorite "runways," or trails. They often take the same trail day after day. Coyotes will leave the runway when they spot something to the side. Then they return to the trail and continue their search for food.

Coyotes will often stop on a ridge or high piece of ground to look for prey. (They also go to high ground to get a better look at their enemies—mainly people.) If they spot prey, they will start their stalk. When they stalk prey, coyotes behave very much like a cat going after a bird. They keep their bodies very close to the ground. They move slowly forward when the prey is looking the other way. When coyotes get within a few feet of their prey, they pounce on it.

Coyotes will only chase prey if they have to do so. They have learned not to waste their energy.

A medium-sized wild dog

The foxes are the smallest wild dogs in North America. Wolves are the largest. Coyotes fit in between.

Adult coyotes usually weigh between twenty and fifty pounds (9 - 23 kg). The average weight is about twenty-five pounds (11 kg). The largest coyote on record weighed seventy-five pounds (34 kg). Most coyotes stand about twenty-four inches (.6 m) tall at the shoulder, and are about four feet (1.2 m) long. Their bushy tails make-up about a third of their length. Female coyotes are usually about twenty percent smaller than the males.

If they aren't killed by people, most coyotes live for eight to ten years in the wild. Some coyotes get to be fifteen years old. The oldest known coyote was eighteen years old when it died in a Washington, D.C. zoo.

The coyote looks very much like a small German shepherd. It has a rather narrow face, with large, pointed ears. It has yellow eyes with round, black pupils. The coyote's nose pad is black.

The shaggy coat of a coyote is mostly reddish-gray in color. The ends of the hairs on its body are tipped with black. There are various dark markings on its head, back, and tail that make each coyote look different. The legs, chin, and belly of the coyote are usually creamy white or buff colored. A few jet-black coyotes have been seen. Experts think that this resulted when a coyote mated with a black dog.

Coyotes that live in desert areas tend to be lighter in color than those that live in brushy or wooded areas. This is nature's way of allowing the coyote to blend with its habitat. Coyotes that live in cold areas will grow a heavy coat of fur for the winter. The winter coat is lighter in color than their summer coat. Again, this allows them to blend better with their snowy habitat. These coyotes will shed their winter coats in the spring, and turn darker in color for the summer.

A varied home range

A coyote travels only as far as it needs to find food. When there is plenty of food, the home range of the coyote is small. The coyote can usually find all it needs within an area of only two to three square miles (5 - 8 sq. k). During the winter, the coyote may have to cover an area that is one hundred square miles (256 sq. k) to find enough food.

When moving about its home range, the coyote usually "dog trots." The coyote can keep up this trot of five to six miles per hour (8 - 10 kph) for hour after hour. When the coyote needs to run, it can average about twenty-five miles per hour (40 kph). In short bursts, the coyote has been known to run as fast as forty miles per hour (65 kph). It is the only wild animal fast enough to catch a jack rabbit.

The coyote is the only predator fast enough to catch a jack rabbit.

CHAPTER THREE:

The breeding season

Like the wolf, the coyote will mate for life. Most coyotes pick a mate when they are about one year old. Some males may not mature enough to mate until their second year. If one mate should die, a new mate is usually chosen.

Coyotes mate during a mid-winter breeding season. In the northern areas of their range, coyotes usually mate in February. They might breed as early as December in the most southern parts of their range. Coyotes that do not already have mates will select a mate during this time.

Building a den

The only time that coyotes use a den is when they are raising pups. Soon after the breeding season, the pair of coyotes that mated will start getting a den ready.

If the pair of coyotes has mated before, they might use the same den that they used last time. Some mates will use the same den year after year. They will only use the den if it has not been disturbed by people. If there is even a hint of danger, the parents will make a new den somewhere else.

New mates have to find a place to make their den. The soil needs to be soft enough so the coyotes can easily dig into the dirt with their paws. Favorite spots are on hillsides, or in the sides of riverbanks, gullies, and canyons.

The parents often dig a long tunnel leading to the den. Tunnels as long as thirty feet (9.1 m) have been found. The den itself usually lies about six feet (1.8 m) under the ground. Sometimes a small hole will be dug to let fresh air into the den. An escape tunnel will often be dug out the back side of the den.

Coyotes often have long tunnels leading to their dens.

If the parents have the time, they may dig one or two other dens nearby. If they are bothered in the first den, the coyotes will move to one of the other dens. Coyotes will sometimes enlarge a den made by foxes, badgers, or skunks.

Raising the pups

The female will carry the young for about two months. When the time to give birth comes near, she will send the male away. The male coyote will now have a big job. He has to hunt for food for both himself and the female. Later he will also have to bring food for the pups.

Female coyotes usually give birth to about six pups. Older females will often give birth to as many as ten pups. The largest litter known had nineteen pups in it. The pups have a good covering of fur, but their eyes are closed when they are born. The pups start to nurse right away. Their eyes will open in about ten days and they will start to crawl around in the den.

The female will start to "wean" the pups when they are about twenty days old. She will start to give them food brought to the den opening by the male coyote. Before giving the food to the pups, the female chews it and swallows it. After awhile, she brings the food back up. It is now soft enough for the pups to eat.

If the coyotes are bothered in any way, they will move the pups to a new den. The female usually carries the pups in her mouth, while the male stands guard.

The pups come out of the den for the first time when they are about one month old. The male now joins the family group for the first time. Both the male and the female play with the pups. Sometimes other coyotes, who don't have pups of their own, will stand watch over the pups while their parents hunt. After awhile, the pups go with their parents on short hunting trips.

By the time the pups are eight or nine weeks old, they are done nursing. The pups are starting to catch some of their own food. Their parents, however, still bring food to the pups. All through the summer, the pups hunt with their parents. The pups are soon catching most of their own food.

By fall, most pups go off on their own. There usually isn't enough food on their parents' home range to

The pups come out of the den when they are about a month old.

During their first summer, pups hunt with their parents.

support the whole family group. If there is plenty of food for the whole group, the pups might hunt with their families until winter.

The pups are in the greatest danger when they do finally go off by themselves. The pups are still learning how to survive in the wild. Some of them have to go a long way before reaching hunting grounds not being used by other coyotes. Some of them are killed by natural enemies, like wolves, cougars, and eagles. Some of the pups are trapped or shot by people.

If the pups get through their first winter, they will be much wiser. Their chances of living to an old age will be much better.

Senses and communication

The coyote uses its sense of smell more than any other sense. It locates dead animals with its nose. The coyote is also more likely to locate rabbits, birds, and small animals with its nose than with its eyes. The coyote uses its sense of smell to detect danger, especially from people. One whiff of human scent, and the coyote will be long gone. The sense of hearing is often used to zero in on an animal that is hiding in weeds and grass. The slightest noise will give away the prey animal. Like all animals that live in open spaces, the coyote also has good eyesight. It uses its eyes to locate food and danger at a distance.

Coyotes have a scent gland at the base of their tails. Each coyote has a different scent. Coyotes use this scent to recognize each other.

To mark their home ranges, coyotes urinate on trees and rocks. They mark the borders of their territory with the urine. Other coyotes will usually stay away if they locate one of these scent markers. It's one of the ways that coyotes use to keep order.

Probably nothing about the coyote is as well-known as its howl. Wherever coyotes live, howling is a regular event each evening. Coyotes go to the highest ground in the area to do their "singing." Their song usually starts with a series of yaps, barks, and whines. This is followed by a long, drawn-out howl. The song usually

Coyotes howl each evening.

ends with a few short yaps. Then other coyotes nearby join in with their own songs.

Experts don't know for sure why coyotes howl. The best they can offer is that coyotes do it to keep in touch with each other. Some experts think that coyotes sometimes howl for the fun of it. Whatever the reason, one thing is for sure. Once you have heard the joyful song of the coyote, you don't easily forget it.

The coyote's enemies

We've already said a great deal about the coyote's biggest enemy—man. There really is not much more that needs to be said. Today, even most ranchers know that the coyote serves the purpose of controlling grass-eating animals. Most of the thoughtless poisoning has stopped. Even when the coyote is hunted today, it's because its fur has value. Man seems to be finally understanding that the coyote is a useful animal to have around.

Besides people, the coyote has to worry about wolves, cougars, and eagles. The predators can kill young coyotes, and even adults. The coyote's worst animal enemy is the family dog. All too often, a pack of pet dogs will get together and start roaming the country-side. They kill many deer and coyotes.

Like other wild animals, the coyote suffers from lice, ticks, mites, and various worms. It also suffers from mange, a disease that causes the coyote to lose its hair. If this happens during the winter, the coyote usually dies. Coyotes can also be killed by distemper and rabies.

The future looks good

In spite of all these dangers, the clever coyote is doing very well. It has learned to live next to man. If we are wise enough, we will learn to always make room for the coyote in our busy world.

Many people now realize that the coyote serves a very useful purpose.

MAP:

The shaded areas show
where most coyotes
live in North America.

INDEX/GLOSSARY:

46

INDEX/GLOSSARY:

WILDLIFE
HABITS & HABITAT

READ AND ENJOY THE SERIES:

If you would like to know more about all kinds of wildlife, you should take a look at the other books in this series.

You'll find books on bald eagles and other birds. Books on alligators and other reptiles. There are books about deer and other big-game animals. And there are books about sharks and other creatures that live in the ocean.

In all of the books you will learn that life in the wild is not easy. But you will also learn what people can do to help wildlife survive. So read on!